MW00966245

# The 3 Relationships Everyone Should Have for Success:

## Mentor, Role Model & Friend

Frank Lee

FRANK LEE

# DEDICATION

I dedicate this first book to my mom and dad, who are always in my corner! My wife and my kids, this is the first book, and this is our legacy. The legacy of the Lee HOUSE OF JUGGAURNATS a force to be reckoned with! My Friend Isaiah, who has pushed me past all my hardships and pressures in life. Thank you and Love you BRUH!!

# CONTENTS

## ACKNOWLEDGMENTS

My Mentors: Dr. Oliver Reid (@YourSolutionCoach), Dr. Fernando Kittrell (@BridgeCrosserChurch). Both of these men have left their mark on my life and so many others. Thank you so much!!
I appreciate you both!

Pastor Jesse and Almeta Radford, you have helped me find my purpose and passion in life, which is helping young people.
I love you both to life.

# INTRODUCTION

## THE 3 RELATIONSHIPS

### A ROLE MODEL
### A MENTOR
### A FRIEND

Throughout my life, I've witnessed a lot of relationships go right, wrong, and be restored. Little did I know, I was noticing the recipe for a successful, strong, joyful, and stable life.

One relationship I've noticed that most successful people have is the person that they look up to or desire to be like. I call them the "go by person". Another person that I have, but a lot of people don't have is the mentor or the wise group. The mentor is a must have. These people must be chosen carefully. Lastly, the running partners are essential. The running partner will be the one that won't let you quit.

Every person in life will have their ups, downs, and times they want to just want to quit and give up. Personally, I have found myself in this position multiple times. In those times, some people have found themselves in a place where they didn't know what to do or who to talk to. They may even be like a "lonely a deer caught in head lights". I don't care who you are, if you are alive, life happens to us all. We all want to be ready as best as we can in life for life. Well, please take a moment to learn these relationships with me and watch some of the life issues you experience change for the better.

The reason for writing this book is because I realized that most people lack wisdom and don't pursue the things they want to do in life. There are many possible reasons why people aren't successful such as, they give up too easily. They think they must do it on their own and they don't finish what they start. This is a huge problem in our culture today for a number of reasons. Another important reason is the lack of the right relationships in their lives. I realized that many in today's society lack a father figure in the home or divorce has taken place in a family.

FRANK LEE

# CHAPTER 1

# THE IMPORTANCE OF A MENTOR

God has a plan for every person on the earth. Unfortunately, scores of people won't come remotely close to it. It's not because God is not able but rather, he doesn't force anyone to do anything. The fact that he doesn't force people to do things causes many to fail to yield to him and his plan. There are several aspects to the will of God. Many don't have a problem with prayer, worship, giving Him thanks, and walking upright. However, there is more to his will. There is a part of his will that requires more of a specific plan and direction for one's life. This is where many falter because they don't understand the multiplicity of God's will as it relates to life goals, objectives, and having a life strategy. To do this we must understand what his will is. The will of God looks different to every person. Just think how weird it would be if everyone did the same exact thing on the earth. God has developed a concept called discipleship to help push, provoke, and challenge individuals to be all that God intends. The Bible speaks of discipleship; however, from the secular standpoint, it is called mentoring. Mentoring is simply discipleship. Look at how the world agrees with God on this. Just because it's called something different, doesn't change what it is.

Some months ago, a woman asked me about how to find a mentor. She also stated that the person that was her present mentor was always tearing her down with negative words. She asked, "Is this normal?" I told her that a mentor is a person in your life that has already attained a level of success in the area that you are striving for. I also shared that, "A mentor builds you up in order for you to accomplish goals." She was amazed because her mentor didn't do any of this. Lastly, I shared with her that "A mentor doesn't have anything to gain from helping you except for the satisfaction that you are growing and achieving." A mentor focuses on your development and not his or her personal gain.

Even the Apostle Paul stated to Timothy, *"I held back nothing that was profitable to you."* (Acts 20:20) A person that tears down your character and leaves you feeling worse than you were, is not the person to tell you anything about growing. God uses mentors to build you in principle, character, and faith to move beyond what seems to be impossible challenges. Mentors are those that have been to and sustained the level of success you are trying to attain. Jesus is the Ultimate Master and Mentor.

He is the greatest of mentors. He gave us an example as to how to influence others with the greatest of skill. Jesus never fussed or hurt people to influence others. The Father's plan had to be carried out and he was going to use ordinary people to do it. So, Jesus now has to mentor or disciple twelve men that would, in turn, reproduce what Jesus imparted in their lives to others. The process simply repeats itself. In fact, I have mentors in my life that I look to. They are older and wiser than myself and have helped me to grow as a person, achieve my goals, and to help others do the same. As a Life Coach, I still need a life coach. As I pour out to others, my mentors pour into me. Be encouraged!

## Here are a few things that you get from a mentor:

1. A mentor can see past your gift, talents, and status and will have the best interest at heart.

2. A Mentor has the wisdom to stop you from going the wrong way.

3. A Mentor won't let you quit because things become too difficult.

4. A mentor looks and listens past your emotion.

## Exodus 18 New Living Translation (NLT)

*Jethro's Visit to Moses*

*18 Moses' father-in-law, Jethro, the priest of Midian, heard about everything God had done for Moses and his people, the Israelites. He heard especially about how the LORD had rescued them from Egypt.*

*2 Earlier, Moses had sent his wife, Zipporah, and his two sons back to Jethro, who had taken them in.*

3 (Moses' first son was named Gershom,[a] for Moses had said when the boy was born, "I have been a foreigner in a foreign land."

4 His second son was named Eliezer,[b] for Moses had said, "The God of my ancestors was my helper; he rescued me from the sword of Pharaoh.")

5 Jethro, Moses' father-in-law, now came to visit Moses in the wilderness. He brought Moses' wife and two sons with him, and they arrived while Moses and the people were camped near the mountain of God.

6 Jethro had sent a message to Moses, saying, "I, Jethro, your father-in-law, am coming to see you with your wife and your two sons."

7 So Moses went out to meet his father-in-law. He bowed low and kissed him. They asked about each other's welfare and then went into Moses' tent.

8 Moses told his father-in-law everything the LORD had done to Pharaoh and Egypt on behalf of Israel. He also told about all the hardships they had experienced

along the way and how the LORD had rescued his people from all their troubles.

9 Jethro was delighted when he heard about all the good things the LORD had done for Israel as he rescued them from the hand of the Egyptians.

10 "Praise the LORD," Jethro said, "for he has rescued you from the Egyptians and from Pharaoh. Yes, he has rescued Israel from the powerful hand of Egypt!

11 I know now that the LORD is greater than all other gods because he rescued his people from the oppression of the proud Egyptians."

12 Then Jethro, Moses' father-in-law, brought a burnt offering and sacrifices to God. Aaron and all the elders of Israel came out and joined him in a sacrificial meal in God's presence.

*Jethro's Wise Advice*

13 The next day, Moses took his seat to hear the people's disputes against each other. They waited before him from morning till evening.

*14 When Moses' father-in-law saw all that Moses was doing for the people, he asked, "What are you really accomplishing here? Why are you trying to do all this alone while everyone stands around you from morning till evening?"*

*15 Moses replied, "Because the people come to me to get a ruling from God.*

*16 When a dispute arises, they come to me, and I am the one who settles the case between the quarreling parties. I inform the people of God's decrees and give them his instructions."*

*17 "This is not good!" Moses' father-in-law exclaimed.*

*18 "You're going to wear yourself out—and the people, too. This job is too heavy a burden for you to handle all by yourself.*

*19 Now listen to me, and let me give you a word of advice, and may God be with you. You should continue to be the people's representative before God, bringing their disputes to him.*

20 Teach them God's decrees, and give them his instructions. Show them how to conduct their lives.

21 But select from all the people some capable, honest men who fear God and hate bribes. Appoint them as leaders over groups of one thousand, one hundred, fifty, and ten.

22 They should always be available to solve the people's common disputes, but have them bring the major cases to you. Let the leaders decide the smaller matters themselves. They will help you carry the load, making the task easier for you.

23 If you follow this advice, and if God commands you to do so, then you will be able to endure the pressures, and all these people will go home in peace."

24 Moses listened to his father-in-law's advice and followed his suggestions.

25 He chose capable men from all over Israel and appointed them as leaders over the people. He put them in charge of groups of one thousand, one hundred, fifty,

*and ten.*

*26 These men were always available to solve the people's common disputes. They brought the major cases to Moses, but they took care of the smaller matters themselves.*

*27 Soon after this, Moses said good-bye to his father-in-law, who returned to his own land.*

Moses is very powerful and has done amazing things led by the Lord. He does something that most of us would not do, but we should. He stopped and honored his father-in-law (mentor). He let him know what was going on and even showed him. His father-in-law saw the great things and was moved by all that God did with them. He looked past all the success and provided a solution that would lighten the load for Moses.

Mentors, it is ok if mentees are doing well. Don't get jealous of them. Give them your wisdom to impact more people. Mentors have a great responsibility to share the wisdom that God has given them so that the people who come behind and under them can go further, run faster, and reach more people. After all the wisdom that you gain through life, it would be a shame to waste it. It won't go anywhere but to the grave, if you don't share it.

**Here's how you can tell you have a great mentor:**

1.    They listen to you.

2.    They don't get in the way of your success.

3.    They add valuable insight that will help you to become more successful.

4.    They don't get jealous of your success.

5.    They want you to continue with what God is doing in your life!

## Your role as a mentee:

1.      Let mentor see and tell them what God is doing.

2.      Listen when they speak.

3.      Take the wisdom and put it to work.

4.      Realize you don't know everything and you need wisdom.

5.      Keep them in your corner and honor them.

Last thing on the mentors. First, you might need to have different mentors for different parts of your life. (Marriage, Finances, business, school. Etc.) If you want to see thing work in different parts of your life find someone that can help you and give you wisdom, so you can keep moving forward.

# Questions for Reflection

1.   Who is a mentor in my life?

_____

_____

_____

_____

_____

## 2. What wisdom can I use from my mentor?

_____

_____

_____

_____

_____

_____

_____

_____

_____

_____

## 3. Does my mentor listen and give you wisdom?

_____

_____

_____

_____

_____

_____

## 4. Can you humble yourself and listen to your mentor? Why or why not?

_____

_____

_____

_____

_____

_____

## 5. What area of your life do you really need a mentor?

_____

_____

_____

_____

_____

_____

_____

_____

_____

# CHAPTER 2

# A FRIEND OR YOUR GO-TO PERSON

L et's face it, at some point or another, we get to a place in life where we question friends and friendships. We think things like, "What's the use of friends?" or "I don't need anyone but myself in life." The truth is, everyone needs a close friend. If humans were meant to be alone, there would be no one here but Adam. So, where do you begin to sort out the pieces that form a close friendship? In actuality, the only way is through circumstances. Not too long ago, I stumbled upon, yet again, one of life's "circumstances." In the next 24 hours, I found myself puzzled and hardly able to put a thought together. Every emotion from sadness to anger and finally defeat coursed through my mind. A family member was in need and I couldn't help them by myself. It didn't take long for me to recognize I needed some assistance. In my case, help was just a phone call away. By the following morning, that call had resulted in a flight scheduled to carry a good friend from Boston to Virginia. Within no time, we greeted each other with laughter and reminisced about memories. We handled the situation at hand and, so it seemed that life was on its way back to its habitual routine. (Or so I thought) As my friend and I caught up on everything we could think of, he interrupted me to say, "Something's not right. You're not you." I'm sure a dumbfounded look rested on my face as a result of that comment. The reality is, I should've expected it. I was going through a few personal trials while trying to meet the demands of friends, coworkers, church members, and family. I hadn't told my friend anything and at the time that he interrupted me, he still didn't know any details. Because our friendship was based on truth and love, he picked up on it very quickly... probably in the airport! From that moment on we would spend countless hours talking, praying, laughing and crying. Slowly, I began to regain my identity and regain my sanity. It was not overnight, but the difference came from a persistent friend; a friend that would not allow me any other option, but progress.

Friends play much more of a vital role in our lives than we often give credit for. Having at least one close friend in your life will make the difference. How do we know that we've found that friend? It appears at every corner, so-called "friends" seem to let you down. The problem that we face that crushes us more than it helps us, is that in today's society our definition of "friend" is incorrect. It is something people use loosely. Once you start to see growth in a relationship, you can rest assured you are on the right track. A friend should always challenge you to grow. There needs to be someone in your corner that sees your potential and is willing to expound on it.

A close friend has to be someone that you can be honest with, in all things and not feel judged. One thing that my friend had to help me break was the brick wall I could assemble in two seconds or less. More times than I can recall, I remember him saying, "It's me. You don't have to be Super Woman." A true friend is going to be the one to be completely honest with you and only to see you become more successful. While we're here on earth, let's use what God has given us to cope with the everyday struggles of life whether big or small. God has given us friends. He has put people in our paths to help us to thrive. With every person, that close friend varies. Maybe it's a parent, sibling, coworker, or classmate, it could be anybody. Whoever this close friend may be in your life, remember to appreciate that friendship.

Why is it so important to have a close friend? Just imagine a life with no one. Imagine going through some of life's hardest lessons and having no one. In the same sense, imagine receiving the greatest news or achieving something remarkable and having no one to share it with. When you look for the quality a close friend holds, keep in mind, you should strive to be that close friend to someone as well. Be ready to be motivated, be ready to succeed, and be ready to be accompanied by that close friend through it all.

# 1 Samuel 19 New Living Translation (NLT)

Saul Tries to Kill David

*1 Saul now urged his servants and his son Jonathan to assassinate David. But Jonathan, because of his strong affection for David,*

*2 told him what his father was planning. "Tomorrow morning," he warned him, "you must find a hiding place out in the fields.*

*3 I'll ask my father to go out there with me, and I'll talk to him about you. Then I'll tell you everything I can find out."*

*4 The next morning Jonathan spoke with his father about David, saying many good things about him. "The king must not sin against his servant David," Jonathan said. "He's never done anything to harm you. He has always helped you in any way he could.*

*5 Have you forgotten about the time he risked his life to kill the Philistine giant and how the LORD brought a great victory to all Israel as a result? You were certainly* happy about it then. Why should you murder an innocent man like David? There is no reason for it at all!"

6 So Saul listened to Jonathan and vowed, "As surely as the LORD lives, David will not be killed."

7 Afterward, Jonathan called David and told him what had happened. Then he brought David to Saul, and David served in the court as before.

8 War broke out again after that, and David led his troops against the Philistines. He attacked them with such fury that they all ran away.

9 But one day when Saul was sitting at home, with a spear in hand, the tormenting spirit[a] from the LORD suddenly came upon him again. As David played his harp,

10 Saul hurled his spear at David. But David dodged out of the way, and leaving the spear stuck in the wall, he fled and escaped into the night.

**Friendships offer you:**

1.      Someone who has your back.

2.      Someone to grow with you.

3.      Someone you unwind with or vent to and they don't judge you but love you.

I'm always watching people that say they don't have friends. Most of the time they might **not** be emotionally stable because they don't have anyone to just unwind and be themselves. A friend knows that you have and cares but doesn't care. They know what you have or don't have but still loves you. They will warn of danger and remind of all the great things you have done. They also know how you are when you are down. Everyone needs a friend that is solid. We all go through times those highs and lows, so share them with your friends.

## Your Responsibility as A Friend:

1.    You must be a good friend in return.

2.    You must have your friend's back.

3.    Love them in return, the way they have loved you.

4.    Be a friend that cares.

5.    Remind your friends how great they are when they are low.

## What to Look for In a Friend:

1.    They want to share life with you.

2.    Both of you can be yourselves around each other.

3.    You can cry in your low times with them.

4.    They don't judge you and tell you the truth in love.

## Questions for Reflection

1.    Are you a good friend? Why or Why Not?

_____

_____

_____

_____

_____

_____

_____

2.    Who are your friends?

_____

_____

_____

_____

_____

_____

_____

3.    What's great about them? Call them and tell them in your own way.

_____

_____

_____

_____

_____

_____

_____

_____

_____

_____

_____

_____

_____

4.     How often do you connect with your friends?

_____

_____

_____

_____

_____

5.     Can you be yourself with your friends? Can they be themselves around you?

_____

_____

_____

_____

_____

_____

# CHAPTER 3

# ROLE MODEL

# (I WANT TO BE LIKE MIKE)

**Luke 9:49 New Living Translation(NLT)**

Using the Name of Jesus

*49 John said to Jesus, "Master, we saw someone using your name to cast out demons, but we told him to stop because he isn't in our group."*

Role models are very important. Why? Because these people help create a vision. They give you something to aim for in life. Role models are in places that you want to be in marriage, finances, business, parenting etc. The Bible says, "The people without a vision will perish!" So, ask yourself, "Where do I want to be?" Then find someone who is there, glean from his or her life, study them, and change your life. Aim to get there!

I have found that most successful people have or has had a role model at some point in time. Role models don't need to be someone you see every day or call. They could be someone on TV, in history, or someone you have interest in. They could also be someone you know. If they happen to be someone you know, ask questions. Find out how they got where they are today. This is very important in your life, so find these people and aim for success!

When I find something I want to do, I look up to those people who are doing it well. Study those people very closely and watch them. See what they are doing and adapt it to fit your life. They have figured out a recipe for success that you can use. These days with social media, we can find information and read about these people very easily. We can look at their hustle, their work ethic and how long it took them to get there.

Most of your role models you might be within reach. Like I said, "they give you a vision where you are going." If you don't have a vision of where you want to go, you will not get there by accident. Live on purpose with a vision of where you want to go. Put in the work and get there.

What I realize about role models is that sometimes they forget others are watching them. When looking at role models please clarify what you like and study that. After all, they still are human beings and just like you and me, they fall short at times.

## Testimony

*Please allow me to introduce myself, I am Vickie M. McBride, a witness, and beneficiary of the commitment of Frank Lee to ministry and his walk with God.*

*I met Frank in 2007 when my family and I began attending Upper Room Christian Cathedral. Frank was involved with the youth in our church and was a terrific leader and role model. More importantly, Frank was an intricate part of my son's re-introduction into society and totally committing his life to Christ.*

*Several years ago, my son became involved in "gang" activity, which eventually landed him in Bon Aire Correctional facility. During his year of incarceration, God had him in a posture in which he could hear his voice. Fortunately, my son took heed to the voice of God and hasn't looked back since. When he returned to society and church, Frank immediately took him under his wing and began to nurture him to spiritual and academic success.*

*Frank spent endless hours with him in Bible study, prayer, and society. During this time, Frank set the standard that my son would follow. Besides mentoring his spiritual walk, Frank took a personal interest in my son's interest to become a gospel rapper. He helped him organize a local group within our church called T.A.G. (This Anointed Generation) and became their manager. With Frank guiding the group, they were able to spread the Word of God through rap – reaching a generation of youth that was lost.*

I put this insert in because sometimes you really don't know who is watching you. Be the best you that you can be for the benefit of others. I love what I do. I love helping people out. I don't do it for anything else, but for the Glory of God. I have been a youth Pastor for a few years and I love the fact that some of those young people still talk about all that was done! It blesses me to know they see that they still do things we did years back. In this case, I was a role model that was reachable.

**Role model** (noun) A person whose behavior, example, or success is or can be emulated by others, especially by younger people.

## Things You Get from A Role Model:

1.  Vision

2.  Valuable lessons

3.  Motivation

4.  Inspiration

## Role Model Duties:

1.  When you realize you are being watched, SHARE.

2.  Don't forget you're human.

3.  Don't forget it's an honor to be considered a role model.

# Questions for Reflection

**1.Who do you look up to? Why?**

_____

_____

_____

_____

_____

**2. What draws you to them?**

_____

_____

_____

_____

_____

_____

**3. What can you take from them? (Methods, tools, traits etc.)**

_____

_____

_____

_____

_____

_____

_____

_____

# 4. How will you adapt and change those things to fit your life?

_____

_____

_____

_____

_____

_____

_____

_____

_____

_____

_____

_____

_____

_____

_____

_____

_____

_____

_____

_____

_____

_____

_____

_____

## CONCLUSION

I have had the privilege to meet a lot of successful people in my life and what I come to learn is that no matter where you are in your life, you will always need these three relationships in your life. I've seen marriages and careers fail because people won't humble themselves and reach out to a mentor. I've seen people who have a lot of money and people who are depressed and can't get out of bed because they don't have friends that they can just be themselves around. I know people who don't have the correct vision for their lives because they don't a great role model to glean from. I have seen many relationships that have become negative. I've seen plenty of people make the most of their lives and achieve success because they have had healthy relationships with role models, mentors, and friends.

Remember, you won't be able to have success in life without people. Anything you do will always include people. Just as you are looking to make these relationships count in your life, there is someone considering you for one of these relationships as well. So, be the best you that you can be!

## ABOUT THE AUTHOR

Frank Lee a husband and father to Amanda, Aryanna, Frank, Aaliyah, and Aalijah. Pastor to some, a friend to a few, and a mentor to many. He is passionate about seeing young people find their purpose and destiny in life. His vision is to charge young people to walk in and carry out their God-given gifts and talents.

84818432R00027

Made in the USA
Middletown, DE
22 August 2018